Primary Ecology Series

The Colors of Nature

Bobbie Kalman

Toronto · Oxford · New York

Crabtree Publishing Company

Primary Ecology Series

Created by Bobbie Kalman

For N-Lynne Paterson

Special thanks to: Christina Doyle (on cover picture), Tania Celest, Michelle Joseph, Marianne Baude, Maria Picard, Bill McBride, Joy Furminger, the students of Michael J. Brennan and Pine Grove Elementary Schools: Stacey Baugaard (on back cover), Stacey Langelaan, Laura Zapata, Jonathan Lau, Darcia Fraser, Erin Yurenko, Hilary Kuzmaski (on title page), Kelvin Bascus, Myroslawa Tataryn, Darrick Yu (on title page), and Brian Bell

Editors
Janine Schaub
David Schimpky
N-Lynne Paterson

Design and computer layout
Antoinette "Cookie" DeBiasi

Artwork and cover design
Antoinette "Cookie" DeBiasi

Cover mechanicals
Rose Campbell

Separations and film
EC Graphics

Printer
Worzalla Publishing

Photographs: Diane Payton Majumdar: pages 5 (top two), 8, 9 (top 3 and bottom left), 10 (top right and bottom), 14 (top), 15, 16, 17 (top), 18, 19 (top), 20 (bottom)
Bobbie Kalman: cover (front and back), title page, pages 4 (both), 11, 20 (top), 22, 23 (bottom left and right), 25 (all), 26
Dave Taylor: pages 9 (bottom right), 17 (bottom), 21, 30 (top)
David Gilchrist: pages 5 (bottom), 10 (top left), 28
Jim Bryant: pages 13 (bottom), 14 (bottom), 19 (bottom), 30 (bottom)
Andre Baude: page 23 (top left)
Marc Crabtree: page 23 (top right)
James Kamstra: pages 12, 13 (top)

Published by
Crabtree Publishing Company

350 Fifth Avenue	360 York Road, RR4,	73 Lime Walk
Suite 3308	Niagara-on-the-Lake,	Headington
New York	Ontario, Canada	Oxford OX3 7AD
N.Y. 10118	L0S 1J0	United Kingdom

Cataloguing in Publication Data
Kalman, Bobbie, 1947-
   The colors of nature

(The Primary ecology series)
Includes index.
ISBN 0-86505-557-2 (library bound) ISBN 0-86505-583-1 (pbk.)
Facts and activities explore the role color plays in the lives of plants, animals, and people.

1. Color - Juvenile literature. 2. Color vision - Juvenile literature.
3. Color variation (Biology) - Juvenile literature. I. Title.
II. Series: Kalman, Bobbie 1947-   . The Primary ecology series

QC495.5.K35 1993   j535.6

Contents

❀ Colors in our world ❀

"Colors make me happy!"

Red, blue, green, yellow, orange, and purple—the world is full of color. When you look around, what colors do you see? Which is your favorite?

Colors are a very important part of nature. Not only do they make the world more beautiful, but they help plants, animals, and people in many interesting ways.

Colors hide both predators and their prey. In the animal world, colors send all kinds of messages, from "Choose me as your mate," to "Don't even think about having me for supper!"

(above) Colorful flowers attract many insects.
(left) Colors help some creatures hide.
(below) Nature's colors are spectacular, even deep in the ocean, where this colorful sea anemone lives!

Light and color

Without light, there would be no color. All colors come from light; color is light! The sunlight we see every day is called **white light**. About three hundred years ago, a scientist named Sir Isaac Newton demonstrated that white light is actually made up of different colors.

Newton's discovery

Newton darkened his room and made a small hole in the shutters. A round beam of sunlight pierced through the hole. He placed a triangular block of glass, called a **prism**, in the path of the sunbeam. The long ray of white light broke up into a band of six colors: red, orange, yellow, green, blue, and violet.

The primary colors of light

The band of colors in light is called the **spectrum**. Red, green, and blue are the **primary** colors of the spectrum. They are the three main colors our eyes can see. All the other colors we know are combinations of these three colors.

A rainbow of colors

Most of the time we cannot see the spectrum, but sometimes it appears as a rainbow. After it rains, the air is filled with moisture. As a ray of sunlight passes through a raindrop, it splits up into its separate colors, just as it did through Newton's prism. Rainbows are also a familiar sight at waterfalls.

sun   prism   spectrum

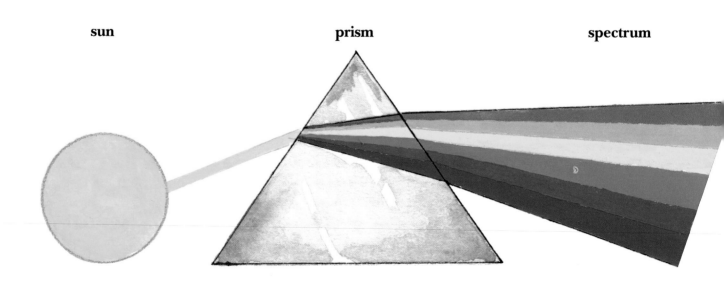

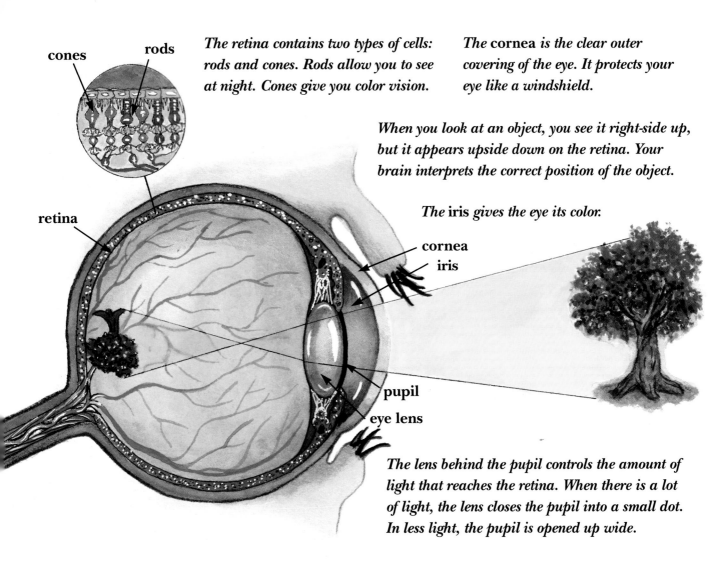

cones

rods

The retina contains two types of cells: rods and cones. Rods allow you to see at night. Cones give you color vision.

The cornea is the clear outer covering of the eye. It protects your eye like a windshield.

When you look at an object, you see it right-side up, but it appears upside down on the retina. Your brain interprets the correct position of the object.

The iris gives the eye its color.

retina

cornea

iris

pupil

eye lens

The lens behind the pupil controls the amount of light that reaches the retina. When there is a lot of light, the lens closes the pupil into a small dot. In less light, the pupil is opened up wide.

❀ How we see ❀

We see with our eyes, but our eyes only work when there is light. Light enters our eye through the **pupil**, the dark round dot at its center. The eye **lens** behind the pupil focuses the light onto the **retina** at the back of the eye. The retina sends signals to the brain, telling us what we are seeing.

Rods and cones

The retina contains millions of tiny cells that help us see. Some of these cells allow us to see when there is very little light. They are called **rods**.

The other types of cells, called **cones**, give us color vision. Not all the cones work in the same way. Some of them see red, some see blue, and others see green. Together, these three types of cones allow us to recognize thousands of colors.

Cones do not see color well in the dark. When there is very little light, everything looks black, gray, and white to us. These are the only colors we see when the lights are turned off at night.

❀ How animals see color ❀

Insects, birds, fish, and reptiles can see color, but most mammals are **colorblind**. Apes, monkeys, and human beings are among the few mammals that can see color.

Infrared vision

Some snakes, such as rattlesnakes, have another way of "seeing." The body heat of animals gives off a light, called **infrared light**, that is invisible to humans. Rattlesnakes can detect this light with special organs below their eyes. Infrared vision helps them find their prey, even in total darkness.

Excellent color vision

Birds have excellent color vision because their eyes contain many cones. Color helps birds recognize their mates, hide their nests, and scare off enemies.

Ultraviolet colors

Wasps and bees can see purple, blue, and yellow flowers well. They can also see **ultraviolet light**. Although this purplish light is a part of sunlight, human beings cannot see it. A flower that looks solid yellow to us may look like a black-lined landing strip to a bee!

(top) A close-up of a frog's eye
(above) The eyes of cats glow in the dark because of an extra layer, called the **tapetum**, *which is behind the retina. The tapetum works like a mirror. It protects the eyes of cats from bright light by reflecting the light back. The tapetum also allows cats to see well in the dark.*
(bottom left) *Bees are able to see ultraviolet markings on flower petals.*

(above) *The eyes of insects are made up of hundreds of long tubes bunched together. Insects are good at spotting movement, but images appear blurry to them.*
(below) *Rattlesnakes find their prey easily in the dark because they can detect the heat given off by animals.*

Whether on land or in the sea, all living creatures get their food energy from plants. Plant-eaters, or **herbivores,** *get it directly, whereas meat-eaters, or* **carnivores,** *such as the cheetahs in the bottom picture, receive energy from plants by eating other animals that have eaten plants. Some animals, called* **omnivores,** *eat both plants and animals. Are you an omnivore or herbivore?*

❀ Green—the color of life ❀

When we think of plants, we think of the color green. Grass, bushes, trees, weeds, leaves, and vines are all green. Even lakes, rivers, and oceans are full of blue-green plants called **algae**.

Green power!

The special **pigment** inside plants that gives them their green color is called **chlorophyll**. Chlorophyll uses the energy of sunlight to change carbon dioxide and water into the food that plants need in order to grow.

The seeds, leaves, fruit, and roots of many plants are eaten by insects, fish,

birds, animals, and people. Plants also give off large amounts of **oxygen**, which cleans the air we breathe. Nothing could survive without plants!

Think green!

What does the word "green" mean to you? Many ecology groups use green as the symbol of a healthy planet. The word "green" can be found on many products sold in stores. "Think green!" slogans remind people to protect the environment. Are you involved in any "green" projects at your school or in your community? Tell your friends and get them involved, too!

❀ Camouflage colors ❀

Have you ever sat quietly and watched the natural world around you? Everything seems perfectly still but, suddenly, a tree branch appears to move. You discover it is not a branch at all—it is a lizard. A cottontail rabbit hops out from under a bush, and a deer mouse scampers across a dead log. You realize that you are not alone. Nature is full of hidden life!

What is camouflage?

For many animals, staying alive depends on blending in with their surroundings. Any shape, color, or pattern that hides or protects is called **camouflage**. Some creatures are so well camouflaged that they are nearly invisible against the background of their habitat.

Predators and prey

Camouflage helps animals hide from their **predator**s. It also helps predators stay invisible so they can sneak up on their **prey**. Camouflage makes it possible for some animals to hunt, but it also allows their prey to escape. It is one of nature's mysterious color tricks!

(above) The frog on the leaf is well camouflaged. Frogs need to stay hidden because they are prey to many birds and reptiles.

(above) The shape and color of the green vine snake match the leaves of this tree almost exactly. (below) These marine iguanas are so well camouflaged that they look like they are a part of the rocky landscape. How many can you count?

(above) Some butterflies and moths blend in with their environment when their wings are folded at rest. When a bird comes too close, however, they can quickly open their wings and reveal their "eye spots," which frighten away birds. (below) The bumps and scales of the land iguana look just like the rocks and vegetation that are found on the Galapagos Islands, where these lizards live.

❀ Special markings ❀

Special markings, textures, and growths also help camouflage animals. Stripes, spots, and bumps can hide animals or frighten away their enemies.

Shapes and patterns

When fawns lie very still, they are well hidden from their predators. Their spotted back blends into the forest floor, which is often dotted with beams of sunlight shining through the treetops. The pattern of spots makes fawns almost invisible!

Growths and textures

Many fish have long, wavy fins that resemble the water plants in which they hide. Alligators look like floating logs in the water. Their rough leathery skin resembles wet tree bark. The body covering of some lizards also has a bumpy texture. It allows them to blend in with both the rocky terrain and vegetation of their habitat.

The pattern on the backs of these baby seagulls matches the rocks in the background.

(opposite) Bees are attracted to yellow and purple flowers. When they collect nectar from one flower, they also pick up pollen and leave it on the next flower they visit. Can you see the pollen on the bee's legs?

❀ Attractive colors ❀

Flowers come in a variety of bright and pale colors. Nature gives them these colors so they can attract insects and birds to their sweet nectar.

Fertilized by insects

When an insect visits a male flower to collect nectar, it picks up a bit of the flower's pollen. That same insect will later land on a female flower and leave some of the pollen that was stuck to its body. The female flower then becomes **fertilized** by the pollen. Fertilized flowers produce the seeds from which new plants will grow.

Bright flowers that bloom during the day attract hummingbirds and insects such as bees, wasps, and butterflies. Flowers that bloom at night have pale colors that are easily seen by night-flying insects such as moths.

Bird colors

Some birds have colorful **plumage** to attract other birds. The color of its feathers tells whether a bird is male or female. Male peacocks have brightly colored feathers, whereas the females have dull-brown ones. The bright colors of some male birds also help lure predators away from a nest. The predator follows the male, and the nest and eggs remain safe.

(above) Baby birds have bright orange or red mouths. The bright color attracts the mother and helps her feed her young. (below) Although most mammals are colorblind, monkeys and apes are not. Male mandrills have multi-colored faces that attract females and frighten away other monkeys.

❀ Watch out! ❀

Insects, mammals, birds, and fish use bright colors and patterns to warn other creatures to stay away. Yellow, black, and red are often the colors of poisonous creatures. The yellow-and-black stripes of bees and wasps warn us that these insects may sting us.

Sometimes non-poisonous animals and insects, such as the spider above, have warning colors to fool their predators.

Red "balloons"

Some lizards and birds have a red throat pouch that inflates like a balloon. This balloon is used to attract females, frighten predators, and keep other males away from a mate.

People also use the warning colors of red and yellow in traffic signals because those are the brightest colors in the spectrum. They easily catch people's attention.

(opposite page and top) The insects shown here have warning colors, patterns, and devices to fool their predators into thinking they are dangerous. How would you react if you met the moth on the opposite page and it was your size? (above) The frigate bird is flying with an inflated pouch. Is he trying to attract a mate or frighten another bird from his territory?

❀ Colors that change ❀

In some parts of the world the amount of sunshine varies from one season to another. Many of the plants and animals that live in these regions change their colors to adapt to the changing climate.

A close-up of an autumn leaf

The colors of autumn

If you live in a cold climate, you witness a dramatic change in the colors of nature each year. In late summer the days grow colder and the air is drier. Trees do not get as much sunshine or water. Everything slows down, and trees stop making food.

When the leaves of trees are not making food, they do not use chlorophyll. Chlorophyll is the pigment that makes leaves green, but there are also red, yellow, and brown pigments in leaves. These other colors start showing through when there is no chlorophyll to cover them up.

Willow ptarmigans have brown spotted feathers in summer, but their feathers are white in winter.

Birds of a feather

In autumn, some northern birds lose their feathers, or **molt**. Their bright summer feathers are replaced by dull-brown ones that match the gray-brown forests of winter.

White for warmth

In the far north, white feathers take the place of the ptarmigan's brown spotted feathers. White feathers blend in with the snowy background. White not only camouflages northern animals in winter, but it also helps them stay warm. Light colors, especially white, keep the heat of the sun much longer than dark colors, even though dark colors absorb heat more quickly.

Quick-change artists

Some animals do not need to wait for a change of season. They alter their colors in the blink of an eye! The most famous of these quick-change artists is the chameleon. Its skin goes from one color to another when there are changes in heat, light, or the colors of its surroundings. Many fish, crabs, and seahorses can also vary their colors to match the colors in the sea.

A chameleon

❀ The color of people ❀

People have different shades of skin, eye, and hair colors. Their body coloring depends mostly on the characteristics they inherit from their parents. If your parents have dark skin, you will also likely have dark skin.

The pigment that makes skin dark is called **melanin**. Melanin helps protect the skin from being burned by too much ultraviolet radiation from the sun. People with dark skin have more melanin than people with light skin.

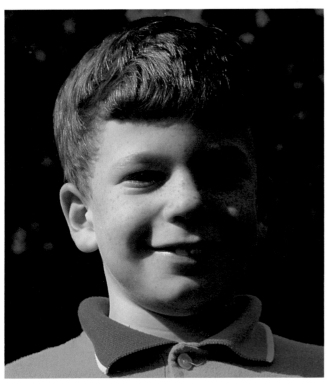

Hair and eye color

People's hair color usually varies with the color of their skin. Those with fair skin can have blonde, red, brown, or black hair. People with darker skin usually have darker shades of hair.

The color of people's eyes can be many shades, from light blue to dark brown. The darker a person's eyes, the more pigment their eyes contain. Brown eyes have a lot of pigment in the iris, whereas blue eyes have much less.

❁ Color activities ❁

Listening, smelling, tasting

We can experience color through many of our senses, not just sight. Try the following experiments:

Hearing color

Pick five colors and ask your classmates to find songs or musical instruments to match the colors. Are their musical choices similar or different than yours? Ask your friends to write down the reasons for each musical choice.

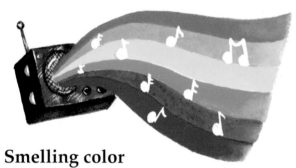

Smelling color

Find five to ten objects that have pleasant or unpleasant odors. Place them on a table and ask your friends to smell each one. What color pops into their mind when they smell each of the objects? Write a poem about color and smell. Give it a funny title such as "Swampy green are my smelly socks!"

Feeling color

Which colors make you feel happy, sad, calm, and cozy? Which do you wear the most? Why are they your favorite colors? Ask your friends to pick a color that best describes their mood today and ask them why they chose that color.

Tasting color

When you taste something spicy, do you think of red? Does a cool glass of water make the color blue pop into your head? Find colors to match things that taste sweet, sour, tart, bitter, and spicy hot. Use interesting colors such as lavender, lime green, and aqua.

Have a color conversation

"*Green-green, green-green!*"
(Telephone rings.)"*Yellow*!"
"Hi *Rose*, it's *Violet*."
"I'm so *plaid* you called! So many *purple* have been getting the *brown* number today."
"I bet it's *Amber* crank-calling. *Orange* you *red* with anger?"
"If she's trying to make me feel *blue*, she's too late. I'm already in a *gray* mood. Got to go."
Pink! (She hangs up.)

Each student has chosen a color to match the sound of a musical instrument. Try this activity using some of your favorite songs. You will have lots of fun!

Christina can see that the flowers are pink, but they feel cool blue to her.

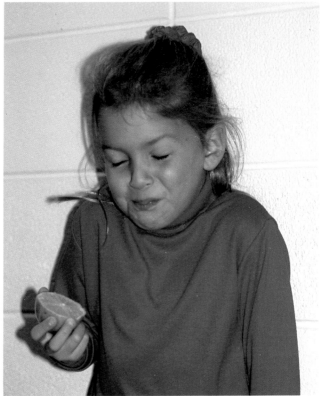

Hilary's face shows how sour the lime tastes. She describes the taste using the color purple.

Do you think the personality descriptions below fit these children and their color choices?

What is your "colorscope?"

Some scientists believe that your color choices may say something about the kind of person you are. Read these colorful descriptions and see if your favorite color matches your personality. Then ask your friends to tell you their favorite color. Do the descriptions fit their personalities well? You decide!

Orange: Orange is cheerful and gets along well with others. Orange people do not like being alone.

Red: Reds are athletic, emotional, and have strong opinions.

Pink: Smart, affectionate people choose pink as their favorite color.

Yellow: Intelligent, original, and serious people love the color yellow.

Green: Lively, fun-loving people like green.

Blue: Are you blue? Blues are conservative, steady, know how to make money, and think before they act.

Purple: Purple people are artistic. They love music and art and want to do things perfectly.

Is your color like mine?

We see as much with our brain as with our eyes. That is why not everyone sees color in the same way. Try this experiment. Paste down ten different colored strips of paper or cloth. With a few friends, go on a color hunt and try to find objects that match each of your color samples. Do you and your friends agree that the colored objects you have chosen match the color strips? Were any of your choices very different from those of your friends?

Designer foods

How would you feel about eating blue chicken soup, purple mashed potatoes, or a green steak? The color of foods affects our attitude towards the meal we are eating. A meal of white fish, white rice, and cauliflower does not excite our appetites, whereas a dinner garnished with colorful vegetables pleases both our stomach and eyes!

With a group of friends, design a menu of colorful, fun foods. Use your imagination! Change the color of familiar foods, put together brightly colored foods, or even choose foods that match your kitchen. Draw pictures of your "designer" meals and write descriptions, such as those found on restaurant menus, that would make others interested in trying your colorful foods.

Which colors do I mix?

When we mix paint, we use red, blue, and yellow to create new colors. If you add white or black, you will get different tints or shades of the colors you make. Experiment with some paint. Which colors will you have to combine to get these colors?

aqua	green	magenta
brown	purple	orange
pink	gray	beige

❀ Colorful facts ❀

Light and dark colors

Dark colors absorb sunlight more quickly than light colors, but light colors trap the heat of the sun for a much longer time. When the sun shines, the earth feels warm compared to the water. When you go swimming at night, however, you will notice the opposite—the water feels much warmer than the ground.

Creatures of light

Insects, animals, and fish come in a variety of colors. We see their colors because sunlight reflects the colors to our eyes. The color of some creatures, however, comes from their own light.

Fireflies have special organs on their abdomen that enable them to glow. Some deep-ocean creatures, such as the arctic jellyfish below, also have their own light sources. The light they produce helps them attract mates and frighten enemies. It also allows them to keep track of one another in the dark ocean water.

Are you colorblind?

Some people cannot tell the difference between certain colors. They are **colorblind**. Men are more likely to be colorblind than women. One male out of every 12 is colorblind, whereas only one female out of 250 is unable to see

all the colors. Does everyone see colors in the same way? What did you learn from the activity at the top of page 27?

Judge it by its color!

Over time, people have learned which foods are poisonous by their color and appearance. The color of meat, fruit, and vegetables can also tell us about their freshness. When meat and cheese turn green, we know that they are unsuitable to eat. Color is a key to ripeness as well. A red blackberry is still unripe, but a raspberry of the same color is delicious! A banana that has turned black is definitely overripe.

Colorful, deadly garbage

Birds, fish, and mammals eat a lot of garbage by mistake because its color resembles the color of their natural foods.

Aluminum tabs from pop cans shimmer and shine like fish. When birds try to swallow them, they choke. Cigarette butts and plastic wrap make animals sick. Helium-filled balloons that escape from children's hands often end up in oceans. Their color washes off, so the balloons look very much like jellyfish. When fish or sea mammals swallow them, they die. Can you imagine all the colorful, poisonous garbage seagulls eat as they search for food at garbage dumps?

Colors of light and paint

The primary colors of light are **red**, **blue**, and **green**, but the colors of pigments and paints are not the same. Primary paint colors are **red**, **blue**, and **yellow**.

When you blend the primary colors of light, these colors are the result.

Mixing the primary colors of paint will result in these colors.

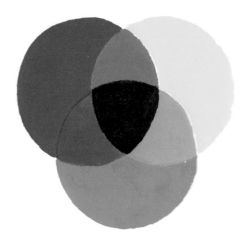

Look at the pictures in this book. Make a list of all the colors you see. How many colors did you write down? Did you know that all those colors were made from red, blue, and yellow? In printing, black is added separately to make pictures look sharper.

❀ Colorful questions ❀

Why do zebras have stripes?

When we think of stripes, many of us think of zebras. Why do these animals have black-and-white stripes when they live among golden grasses?

Over the years, scientists have offered several explanations. Some felt that the stripes distract predators, giving

zebras a few seconds to escape. Others said that the stripes help zebras stay cool in the hot sun and keep insects away. Scientists now feel that the only reason zebras have stripes is that the stripes attract other zebras. Do you believe this latest theory? Why do you think zebras have stripes? Write a serious or funny explanation using a zebra's point of view.

Boobies with blue feet?

There is a variety of seabird called a booby. Some boobies have masked faces and some have red feet. The boobies that are very different from other birds, however, are the blue-footed boobies. Why do they have blue feet? Well, why not!

❀ Glossary ❀

adapt To adjust oneself to new conditions

algae Simple, tiny plants that grow in water. Seaweeds are types of algae.

booby A seabird with red or blue feet

camouflage Any color, shape, or pattern that hides or protects

carbon dioxide A colorless, odorless gas that plants use to make food

carnivore A flesh-eating animal

chameleon A lizard that has the ability to change color

chlorophyll The green substance found in plants that changes carbon dioxide and water into plant food and oxygen

colorblindness A limited ability to distinguish between colors

environment The surroundings that affect the lives of people and animals

fertilize To provide a female flower with pollen

frigate bird A large sea bird

Galapagos Islands Islands located off the coast of Ecuador in South America

herbivore A plant-eating animal

infrared light Light waves invisible to the human eye that are given off by heat

mammals Warm-blooded animals, including humans, that have a backbone and hair. Female mammals give birth to live young and are able to feed their babies with their own milk.

melanin The pigment that makes skin dark

molt To shed skin, feathers, or hair that will be replaced by new growth

nectar The sweet liquid in flowers

pigment A natural substance that colors the cells or tissues of living things

omnivore A living being that eats both plants and animals

oxygen A colorless, odorless gas necessary for breathing

plumage The feathers of a bird

pollen A fine powder on the male parts of flowers that fertilizes the female parts of flowers

predator An animal that hunts other animals

prey An animal that is hunted by other animals

primary First in order or importance

prism A triangular piece of glass that is used to break white light into its separate colors

reptile A cold-blooded, air-breathing animal such as a snake, lizard, or turtle

sea anemone A sea animal with a tubelike body, brightly colored tentacles, and a mouth at one end

slogan An often-repeated word or phrase used by a group of people

spectrum A band of light that has been broken up into six colors: red, orange, yellow, green, blue, and violet

tapetum A protective layer found in the eyes of cats and sharks that reflects light away from the eye

ultraviolet light Purplish light waves that are not visible to the human eye

❀ Index ❀

1 2 3 4 5 6 7 8 9 0 Printed in the U.S.A. 2 0 1 9 8 7 6 5 4 3